Note Speller

by FRED WEBER

A SYSTEMATIZED SET OF WORK SHEETS
FOR SUPPLEMENTING ANY ELEMENTARY CLASS OR PRIVATE METHOD.

DESIGNED TO HELP THE STUDENT GAIN A BETTER UNDERSTANDING OF THE PROBLEMS
OF FINGERING AND READING MUSIC AND AT THE SAME TIME SAVE VALUABLE LESSON TIME.

Published for:
Flute and Piccolo (EL00462)
Clarinet (EL00448)
Oboe (EL00463)
Bassoon (EL00464)
Saxophone (EL00451)

Trumpet (Baritone T.C.) (EL00449)
French Horn (EL00465)
Trombone (EL00450)
Baritone B.C. (EL00467)
Tuba (EL00468)
Drum Rhythm Speller (EL01063)

HOW TO READ THE CHART (Page 3)

● – means put valve down.

○ – means not to put valve down.

When two notes are given together on the chart page 3 (F♯ and G♭), they are the same tone and of course played with the same fingering.

Elementary Fingering Chart

In order to make the fingering chart as easy to understand as possible, only those fingerings necessary in the elementary phase of cornet playing are given.

LESSON 1

You should know the following.

Staff   Bar   Double bar   Measure   Clef sign   Time signature

1 **Match the symbols in the TOP line with their names.**
The first one is done for you.

1-Staff; 2-Measure; 3-Clef sign; 4-Bar; 5-Time signature; 6-Double bar.

2 The Treble Clef sign (𝄞) is usually found at the beginning of each staff of clarinet music.
There are 3 easy steps in learning to draw this sign.

a - Step 1-A straight line extending above and below the staff.

Step 2-A curved line that crosses the up and down line on the 4th line of the staff.

Step 3-A curved line touching the bottom line and the 3rd line as above.

b - Draw 3 lines as in step one above.

Draw the 3 curved lines as in step 2 above.

Complete the curve as in step 3 above.

Draw 3 complete Treble Clef signs.

LESSON 2

1 a - Put names of notes in squares above the staff.
b - Fill in dots for valves to be used to play the note.
Note: Valves are numbered as follows: 1 2 3
                                     0 0 0

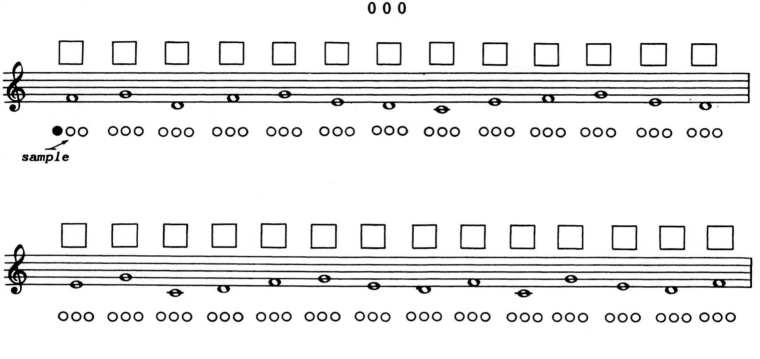

sample

2 Put the number of the line or space the note is on, in the square and write below
whether the note is on a line or space.

1	3										
space	line										

LESSON 3

1 a - Put notes called for on the staff.
b - Fill in dots for valves to be used to play the notes.

2 Draw on the staff.

| Whole note | Half note | Treble clef sign | Time signature | Double bar | Whole rest |

| Half rest | Time signature | Double bar | Bar | Half note | Treble clef sign |

| Whole rest | Whole note | Time signature | Half rest | Bar | Half note |

LESSON 4

1 a - Write different notes for the fingering indicated. (Use only notes you have learned).
   b - Give names of all notes.

2 a - Put notes on the lines and spaces as called for.
   b - Put names of notes in the boxes.

LESSON 5

1 a - Put names of notes in squares above staff.
 b - Mark valves.

2 What are the names of notes on the following lines and spaces?

1 - 1st line - $\boxed{E}$	11 - 4th line - ☐
2 - 2nd space - ☐	12 - 3rd line - ☐
3 - 5th line - ☐	13 - 1st line - ☐
4 - 4th space - ☐	14 - 1st space - ☐
5 - 3rd line - ☐	15 - 5th line - ☐
6 - 2nd line - ☐	16 - 1st space - ☐
7 - 3rd space - ☐	17 - 2nd space - ☐
8 - 5th line - ☐	18 - 2nd line - ☐
9 - 4th space - ☐	19 - 3rd line - ☐
10-2nd line - ☐	20 - 4th space - ☐

LESSON 6

1 a – Put notes called for on the staff. (Use notes you have learned).
   b – Mark fingerings.

2 a – Match the **Notes** on the staff with the rest, or rests, receiving the same number of counts.

b – Match the **Rests** on the staff with the note receiving the same number of counts. (In 4/4 time).

LESSON 7

1 **Match the Symbols on the staff with their names.**
The first one is done for you.

1 - Sharp	5 - Clef Sign	9 - Half note
2 - Tie	6 - Whole note	10- Flat
3 - Bar	7 - Quarter rest	11- Quarter note
4 - Time Signature	8 - Natural sign	12- Half rest
		13- Whole rest

2 **Give the number of counts the notes and rests receive in 4/4 time.**

3 **Write the counting in the measures below. The first measure is done for you.**
Always remember to think the number of the count when playing.

1 2 3 4

LESSON 8

1 a - Put names of notes in squares.
   b - Mark fingering.

2 A Tie combines 2 or more notes on the same line or space.
   A Slur is a curved line that looks like a tie but it joins groups of notes on different lines and spaces.
   Mark the ties below with a T and slurs with an S.

LESSON 9

1 The following notes spell words. What are they?

--- --- --- --- --- --- --- --- --- --- --- ---

--- --- --- --- --- --- --- --- --- --- --- ---

2 Write the following words on the staff.
Where you have learned two notes with the same name - write the lowest one.

F A D E   B A D G E   C A F E   D A D   A B E   D E A D   C A B

B E G G E D   B E D   C A B B A G E   A G E   F A D E D

3 Write the counting under the following measures.

1 2 3 4

LESSON 10

1 a - Put the notes called for on the staff.(Use notes you have had in your lessons).
b - Mark fingerings.

2 Write T under the notes that should be tongued and S under those that should be slurred. Tongue only the first note of each slur.

3 Write the note receiving the number of counts called for in 4/4 time.

E.L. 449

LESSON 11

1 a – Write different notes for the fingerings given.
 b – Name the notes.

2 Three of the most common kinds of time are 4/4; 3/4; & 2/4.
   4/4 means there are 4 counts in each measure.
   3/4 means there are 3 counts in each measure.
   2/4 means there are 2 counts in each measure.
Put the correct time signature at the beginning of each measure.

3 Write the counting under the measures below.

   1 2 3 4

LESSON 12

1   a – Name the notes.
      b – Mark fingering.

2 Add the time received by the notes, in 4/4 time, and put the total in the square.

𝅝 + 𝅗𝅥 + 𝅗𝅥 = ☐   𝅝 + 𝅗𝅥. + 𝅝 = ☐

𝅘𝅥 + 𝅗𝅥. + 𝅘𝅥 = ☐   𝅗𝅥. + 𝅗𝅥 + 𝅘𝅥 = ☐

𝅝 + 𝅗𝅥 + 𝅘𝅥 = ☐   𝅘𝅥 + 𝅘𝅥 + 𝅗𝅥. = ☐

𝅘𝅥 + 𝅝 + 𝅗𝅥. = ☐   𝅘𝅥 + 𝅘𝅥𝅮 + 𝅗𝅥. = ☐

𝅘𝅥 + 𝅘𝅥 + 𝅗𝅥 = ☐   𝅘𝅥 + 𝅝 + 𝅘𝅥 = ☐

3 Match the following.

D . C.   – ☐   1 – The end

Fine   – ☐   2 – Repeat

𝄇   – ☐   3 – Go back to the beginning

𝄐   – ☐   4 – 4/4 time

C   – ☐   5 – Give extra time (hold).

E.L. 449

LESSON 13

1 a – Write the notes on the staff (always use the highest note you have learned unless it tells you to do otherwise).

b – Mark the fingering for the notes you have written.

2 In the measures below is the Second note Higher; Lower; or the Same as the First note?

3 On the top staff is a series of notes and rests. You are to rewrite this line on the bottom staff changing notes to rests of the same time value and rests to notes of the same time value.

sample   etc.

LESSON 14

1   a - Name the notes.
      b - Mark the fingerings.

2 a - Write the letter name of the Sharps. (A Sharp is on the line or space that passes through the center (♯) of the Sharp.)

A♯ _ _ _ _ _ _ _ _ _ _ _ _ _ _ _ _ _ _ _

    b - Write the letter name of the Flats. (A Flat is on the line or space that passes through the center (♭) of the Flat.

_ _ _ _ _ _ _ _ _ _ _ _ _ _ _ _ _ _

3 Write the counting under the measures below.

1 2 3 4

E.L. 449

LESSON 15

1   a - Write the full names of the notes.
   b - Mark the fingerings.

2   a - Put in the Bar lines. (Note Time signatures).
   b - Write the counting under each measure.

LESSON 16

1 A flat or sharp remains in effect throughout the entire measure unless cancelled by a natural (♮).

In the examples below—is the Third note like the First, Second or Both?

2nd ___ ___ ___ ___

___ ___ ___ ___ ___

2 Put the following on the staff below:

1 - Sharp   6 - Natural sign
2 - Half note   7 - Flat
3 - Clef sign   8 - Whole rest
4 - Time signature   9 - Half rest
5 - Quarter rest   10-Dotted half note

1   2   3   4   5   6   7   8   9   10

3 Write on the staff.

F♯   E♮   C♯   B♭   F♮   E♭   C♮   B♮   D♯   G♯   A♭   D♭

E.L. 449

LESSON 17

1 a - Write different notes for the fingerings given.
   b - Name the note you have written.

2 Complete the Time signatures.

3 Put in Bar lines and write counting under each measure.

LESSON 18

1 Add the time of the notes and rests in 4/4 time.

2 Answer Yes or No to the questions below.

Is the last
note like the
1st note?____

Is the last
note like the
2nd note?____

Is the last
note like the
3rd note?____

Is the last
note like the
1st note?____

Is the last
note like the
1st note?____

Is the last
note like the
1st note?____

Is the last
note like the
1st note?____

Is the last
note like the
1st note?____

Is the last
note like the
1st note?____

Is the last
note like the
1st note?____

3 a – Put in Bar lines. (Note Time signatures).
b – Write T under the notes that should be tongued and S under those that are not tongued.

LESSON 19

1 a - Name the notes.
   b - Mark the fingering.

2 Circle the notes affected by the key signatures. When we have one flat in the key signature it is always B♭.

When we have one sharp in the key signature it is always F♯.

3 On what count do the following examples start?

___   ___   ___   ___   ___

E.L. 449

LESSON 20

1 a - Write 2 B♭'s and give
     fingering.

b - Write 2 F♯'s and give
     fingerings.

c - Write 2 E♭'s and give
     fingerings.

d - Write 2 C♯'s and give
     fingerings.

2 Circle the notes affected by the key signatures. When we have 2 flats they are always
    B♭ & E♭.

    When we have 2 sharps they are always F♯ & C♯.

3 Add notes or rests to the measures below so each measure contains the correct number of counts.

LESSON 21

Eighth Notes

We have had drill using 4 kinds of notes and rests.

o - whole note;   ▭ - whole rest;   = 4 counts

♩. - dotted half note; - - - - - - - - - - - = 3 counts

♩ = half note;   ▭ - half rest;   = 2 counts

♩ - quarter note;   𝄾   - quarter rest;   = 1 count

From now on our work will include eighth notes. The eighth note gets only one half count and it takes two of them to make one count. In other words, two eighth notes are played on one count.

A single eighth note looks like this - ♪

When we have two together on one
count they are joined like this   - ♫

This is an eighth rest   - 𝄾

1 In the measures below, on what count do we play the eighth notes?

—————   —————   —————   ——— & ———   ——— & ———

2 Put in the Bars and write counts.

3 a - Complete the Time signature.
b - Write counting under each measure.

LESSON 22

1   a - Make the following notes one half step higher. Be sure you consider the
"Key Signature"

     b - Make the following notes one half step lower. Be sure you consider the
Key signature.

2 Sometimes we have different names for the same tone. For instance E♭ and D♯ are the same tone. These notes are called Enharmonic Tones. The following rule applies in most cases (except between B & C; E & F).

         One note sharped is the same as the noted above flatted.

         One note flatted is the same as the note below sharped.

On the staff below write another note that is the same as the given note.

sample

E.L. **449**

Name of Student_____

26

LESSON 23

1 Join the stems on the notes below so you have the correct number of counts in each measure. The first measure is done for you.

Sample

2 a - Complete the measures below with either notes or rests. (Note Time signature).

3 a - Put in Measure bars. (Note Time signature).
b - Write counting under each measure.

LESSON 24

In this story the missing words are spelled in notes. Fill in the blanks and you will have the complete story.

A Day at the Zoo

Mary Jane, and Dickie packed their _____, washed their _____s, bade mother

and _____ goodbye and took a _____ to the zoo. They first saw

the _____ old lion in his _____. They next _____ the _____ tiger

and _____ him some _____. The monkeys _____ for peanuts.

This _____ fun to their visit. As the light of day   and

the sun _____ in the west they took another _____ and hurried home.

Circle the notes that are affected by the key signature.

Write counting under each measure.

LESSON 25

1 Make each note either one half step higher or lower as indicated. H means higher; L means lower. <u>Warning</u> - Be sure you take the Key signature into consideration. The first one is a sample.

H L L L H L H L L L H

H L H H H L L H L L H H H

2 a - Write the notes below one Octave lower.

etc.

b - Write the notes below one Octave higher.

etc.

LESSON 26
A Camping Trip

_____ and _____ , _____ 10, _____their _____to take them

on a camping trip. They promised not to be _____ so in return for

several good _____s their _____ hired __ _____for a small

_____ to take them to a camp at the _____ of the forest. Their

_____included several _____ shirts and __ blanket for their _____

Their _____ packed the food and mother _____ some _____, _____

and __ dozen _____s. ___ Wore his merit _____ and _____ his

_____belt. ___, _____ and their _____ _____goodbye to mother

and were off.

Speed Test Number 1

Name the notes. Work for speed. Each test should be completed in 1 min. and 30 seconds or less. When completed turn the page upside down and try again.

Seconds

Time

Speed Test Number 2

Write notes above letter names - Time limit 1 min. and 30 seconds. Use different octaves.

Seconds

Time

A C G D B E F A A F D E B C G

B C D A G B D E F G A C D F E

C D A G E E F B C D E F A D C

G A B D B C D F C E A C G A B

Speed Test Number 3

Name notes - Time limit - 1 min. and 30 seconds. Turn paper upside down and name for additional practice.

_____ **Seconds**
        Time

Speed Test Number 4

Write the notes above the letter names - Time limit 1 min. and 30 seconds. Use different octaves.

_____ **Seconds**
        Time

A   C   D   F   A   E   C   B   G   B   A   C   D   E   F

G   D   C   B   A   C   E   A   F   G   E   B   D   F   G

C   D   F   G   A   C   B   D   E   B   F   A   G   B   E

D   C   A   F   A   G   B   C   F   E   C   E   B   D   G

Glossary

1. ≡ staff.

2. 𝄞 - treble clef sign.

3. 𝄢 - bass clef sign.

4. 4/4 - time signature.

5. ≡ bar.

6. ≡ double bar.

7. ≡ measure.

8. ♭ - flat - lowers a note a 1/2 step.

9. ♯ - sharp - raises a note 1/2 step.

10. ♮ - natural - cancels a sharp or flat.

11. ≡ leger lines.

12. ≡ tie.

13. ≡ slur.

14. C - common time. (Same as 4/4 time)

15. ‖: :‖ repeat section between two sets of dots.

16. D.C. - Da Capo - go back to beginning.

17. D.S. - Del Segna - go back to sign (𝄋).

18. Fine - finish - the end.

19. ⌢ - hold or fermata - give extra time.

20. ⁒ - repeat preceding measure.

21. ‖1 ‖2 1st and 2nd endings. Play 1st ending the first time - then repeat strain and play 2nd ending the second time.

22. ⊕ - coda sign - go to coda.

23. 𝄋 - sign.

24. Key Signature - Flats or sharps placed at the beginning of each line to indicate certain notes that are to be sharped or flatted.

25. pp - pianissimo - very soft.

26. p - piano - soft.

27. mp - mezzo piano - moderately soft.

28. mf - mezzo forte - moderately loud.

29. f - forte - loud.

30. ff - fortissimo - very loud.

31. < - increase volume.

32. > - decrease volume.

33. rit. - ritard - gradually slower.

34. rall. - rallentando - gradually slower.

35. accel. - accelerando - gradually faster.

36. cresc. - crescendo - gradually louder.

37. dim. - diminuendo - gradually softer.

38. Chromatic scale - a scale that progresses by half steps.

39. ¢ - alla breve, or cut time.

40. > - accent mark - play with force.

41. simile - continue in similar manner.

42. ♩ - staccato - short and repeated.

43. ♪♪♪ - triplets - three notes played in the time of two.